The Principles of Vision:

The Ray Dalio Story

MICHEAL HOLMES

TABLE OF CONTENTS

CHAPTER ONE

EARLY YEARS AND EDUCATION

The Beginnings of a Future Titan

In a modest neighborhood of Queens, New York, amidst the hustle and bustle of post-war America, a child was born who would grow to become one of the most influential figures in the world of finance. Ray Dalio, born on August 8, 1949, entered a world rapidly transforming, a perfect crucible for a mind inclined towards understanding patterns and change.

A Family Grounded in Music and Values

Ray's early life was framed by the musical career of his father, Marino Dallolio, a jazz musician, and the steadfast support of his homemaker mother, Ann. His Italian heritage played a subtle but significant role in shaping his values and work ethic. The family, though not wealthy, was rich in culture and values, instilling in young Ray an appreciation for hard work and the arts.

Education: A Foundation for Critical Thinking

Dalio's education began in a local public school, where he was an ordinary student, more interested in the happenings of the world outside than the confines of a classroom. His curiosity was piqued not by textbooks but by the process of learning itself and the broader world. This trait would become a cornerstone of his future success.

In high school, Ray showed an early interest in the stock market. His first investment was in Northeast Airlines at the age of 12, funded by his earnings as a golf caddy. This early foray into investing was not just a financial endeavor but an exercise in understanding and predicting patterns, a skill he would continue to refine.

College Years: Shaping a Worldview

Dalio's journey took a significant turn when he attended Long Island University's C.W. Post campus, where he studied finance. It was here that the early foundations of his investment philosophy began to take shape. He was drawn to the dynamic and challenging world of the stock market, seeing it as a puzzle to be deciphered.

During his college years, Ray was deeply influenced by the era's tumultuous economic and political climate. The late 1960s and early 1970s were marked by significant events such as the Nixon Shock and the oil crisis, which played a pivotal role in shaping his understanding of economic principles and global markets.

The Birth of an Investor

Upon graduating in 1971, Ray pursued an MBA from Harvard Business School. Harvard provided not just an education in finance but a network and a broader perspective on the world. It was here that Dalio's thoughts on risk, reward, and economic patterns crystallized, laying the groundwork for what would eventually become Bridgewater Associates.

The Prologue to Greatness

As he stepped out of Harvard, armed with education, a unique worldview, and an unquenchable thirst to understand the world's financial systems, Ray Dalio was on the brink of starting a journey that would not just define his life but also leave an indelible mark on the world of finance.

CHAPTER TWO

THE BIRTH OF BRIDGEWATER ASSOCIATES

Humble Beginnings

In 1975, the seeds of what would become the world's largest hedge fund were sown, not in the bustling streets of Wall Street but in a two-bedroom apartment in New York. Ray Dalio, armed with his Harvard MBA and a stint at the New York Stock Exchange, embarked on an audacious journey to create a different kind of investment firm. Bridgewater Associates, named after an area in Westchester where Dalio had caddied as a boy, began as a small advisory service.

A Visionary's Struggle

The early days of Bridgewater were marked by struggles typical of any new venture. Dalio juggled multiple roles, from being the chief strategist to handling client relations and managing operations. The company initially provided institutional investment advisory services, but Dalio's vision was larger. He aimed to apply his deep understanding of economics, his unique principles, and his growing insights into how the world economy worked.

The Transition

In the late 1970s and early 1980s, Bridgewater Associates slowly began to evolve. Dalio's reputation as a shrewd analyst of global financial markets grew, attracting more clients and more complex challenges. It was during this period that Dalio started developing the unique investment strategies that would later become synonymous with Bridgewater's success.

Embracing a Global Perspective

Dalio's approach was distinguished by its global macro-economic perspective. He believed in understanding the world as an interconnected system, a belief that drove him to study and predict global economic trends. His approach wasn't just about numbers and data; it was about understanding the political, social, and economic fabric that drove markets.

Early Successes and Setbacks

Bridgewater's early successes were remarkable but not without setbacks. Dalio's unorthodox methods and bold predictions sometimes led to skepticism among peers. However, it was his ability to learn from failures and his unwavering belief in his principles that kept him and Bridgewater afloat.

Bridgewater's Philosophy Takes Shape

During this transformative period, the core philosophy of Bridgewater began to take shape. This philosophy was not just about investment strategies but about the culture of the workplace. Dalio was fostering an environment of radical transparency and open-mindedness, which would later become the bedrock of Bridgewater's culture.

Conclusion: The Dawn of a Giant

11

By the end of the 1980s, Bridgewater Associates had established itself as a respected entity in the investment world. The small firm that started in an apartment had begun its journey towards becoming a giant, not just in size but in its approach to investing and workplace culture. This chapter marked the end of just the beginning for Ray Dalio and Bridgewater Associates. The subsequent chapters will delve into the development of Dalio's investment philosophies, the meteoric rise of Bridgewater, and the challenges and successes that lay ahead.

CHAPTER THREE

DEFINING MOMENTS OF GROWTH AND PHILOSOPHY

The Rise to Prominence

As the 1990s dawned, Bridgewater Associates, under Ray Dalio's leadership, began to climb the ranks of the financial world. The firm's assets under management grew, and so did its influence. This period was crucial in solidifying Bridgewater's reputation as a leading investment firm.

Innovations in Investment Strategy

Dalio's approach to investment was both innovative and unconventional. He developed the 'Pure Alpha' strategy, focusing on seeking out uncorrelated returns, betting on both rising and falling markets. This strategy was predicated on deep analyses of economic patterns and global monetary policies, distinguishing Bridgewater from its peers.

Bridgewater's Culture: Radical Transparency and Meritocracy

A significant part of this chapter is dedicated to the unique culture Dalio fostered at Bridgewater. The concept of 'radical transparency' was revolutionary, where employees were encouraged to openly challenge ideas, regardless of hierarchy. This approach, while controversial, was credited with fostering an environment of innovation and critical thinking.

The All Weather Strategy

Another milestone in this period was the development of the 'All Weather' investment strategy. This risk-balanced approach was designed to perform well across different economic environments, further cementing Bridgewater's reputation for innovative and sound investment philosophies.

Global Economic Insights

Dalio's insights into the global economy became highly sought after during this period. His understanding of economic cycles, debt crises, and currency markets made him a respected voice in international finance circles. This influence was not limited to investment strategy but extended to shaping how global economic trends were understood.

Challenges and Criticisms

As the firm grew in size and influence, it also faced criticisms, especially related to its unique work culture and Dalio's leadership style. The firm's methodologies, though successful, were often seen as unconventional and sometimes controversial.

Establishing a Legacy

By the late 1990s, Bridgewater Associates had not only grown in terms of assets and influence but had also begun to leave a lasting impact on the world of finance. Ray Dalio's philosophies and the firm's unique culture were not just defining Bridgewater but were also starting to influence how other organizations approached finance, investment, and corporate culture.

CHAPTER FOUR

TRIUMPHS AND TURBULENCE

Navigating the Dot-Com Bubble

As the new millennium dawned, the financial world was rocked by the bursting of the dot-com bubble. Bridgewater Associates, under Ray Dalio's leadership, managed to navigate these turbulent waters with remarkable foresight. The firm's strategies, which emphasized diversification and understanding economic cycles, proved effective in mitigating the crisis's impact.

The 2008 Financial Crisis

A significant focus of this chapter is on the 2008 global financial crisis. Dalio's deep understanding of debt cycles and economic patterns enabled Bridgewater to not only foresee the crisis but also to position itself advantageously. This period highlighted Bridgewater's resilience and the strength of its investment strategies, as it was one of the few firms to record positive returns during the crisis.

Expansion and Global Impact

The early 2000s also marked a phase of expansion for Bridgewater. The firm's success during the financial crisis bolstered its reputation, attracting more clients and leading to significant growth in assets under management. Bridgewater's influence extended beyond Wall Street, shaping economic policies and decision-making in financial institutions worldwide.

Philosophical Dissemination

Ray Dalio began to focus on disseminating his philosophies and insights during this period. His public speaking engagements and publications, including his later book 'Principles,' articulated his life and management principles, attracting attention far beyond the financial world.

Cultural Controversies

However, the firm's culture of radical transparency and its unorthodox management practices also drew criticism. This period saw increased public scrutiny and debates over the work environment at Bridgewater, with some former employees describing it as challenging and intense.

The Role of Technology

Bridgewater's embrace of technology in investment strategies. Dalio's interest in algorithmic trading systems and data-driven decision-making processes marked a significant evolution in the firm's approach to investment management.

A Firm That Redefined Finance

By the end of the first decade of the 21st century, Bridgewater Associates had firmly established itself not just as a financial titan but as an entity that had profoundly influenced the world of finance. The firm's triumphs during economic downturns, coupled with its philosophical and technological advancements, set the stage for its continuing evolution in the years to follow.

CHAPTER FIVE

DALIO'S EXPANDING INFLUENCE

The Publication of "Principles"

A pivotal moment in Ray Dalio's career came with the publication of his book, "Principles," which encapsulated his life and work philosophies. This book, which became a bestseller, extended his influence beyond the financial world, positioning him as a thought leader in areas of management, psychology, and personal development.

Bridging Finance and Technology

This chapter also explores how Bridgewater, under Dalio's guidance, continued to innovate at the intersection of finance and technology. The firm invested heavily in algorithmic trading and machine learning, integrating these technologies into its investment strategies and operational processes.

Global Economic Forecasting

Dalio's role as a global economic forecaster became more pronounced. His analyses of debt cycles, currency markets, and economic policies were increasingly sought after by policymakers and business leaders worldwide. His ability to predict economic trends with a high degree of accuracy further bolstered his reputation as a visionary thinker.

Philanthropy and Social Engagement

Dalio's foray into philanthropy and social engagement marked a new chapter in his career. His initiatives focused on education, ocean exploration, and mental health, reflecting his broader interests and commitment to societal well-being. This shift also illustrated a more holistic approach to his legacy, extending beyond financial success.

Critiques and Challenges

The chapter doesn't shy away from the critiques and challenges faced by Dalio and Bridgewater. The intense scrutiny of

Bridgewater's internal culture continued, and Dalio's public statements and predictions were not without their detractors. This period was a testament to the complex interplay between success, public perception, and the burdens of leadership.

Mentoring the Next Generation

Dalio's role in mentoring the next generation of leaders and thinkers at Bridgewater and beyond is a significant focus. His commitment to sharing his knowledge and experiences was evident in his interactions with young entrepreneurs, economists, and business leaders.

A Multifaceted Legacy in the Making

By the mid-2010s, Ray Dalio had firmly established himself as a multifaceted figure: a successful financier, a thought leader, a technology enthusiast, and a philanthropist. His journey from a Wall Street maverick to a global influencer encapsulated a journey of continual learning, adaptation, and a desire to impact the world positively.

CHAPTER SIX

BRIDGEWATER'S ADAPTATION AND DALIO'S LEGACY

The Changing Landscape of Global Finance

The rapidly evolving landscape of global finance in the latter half of the 2010s. Bridgewater Associates, under Ray Dalio's stewardship, faced new challenges and opportunities in this dynamic environment. The firm had to navigate geopolitical shifts, emerging markets, and the increasing influence of technology in finance.

Embracing Innovation and Sustainability

Dalio's vision led Bridgewater to embrace innovative strategies that integrated sustainability and environmental considerations into their investment processes. This shift was not only a response to the changing market demands but also reflected Dalio's growing concern for global environmental issues and sustainable economic growth.

The Rise of Artificial Intelligence in Finance

A significant portion of the chapter is dedicated to exploring Bridgewater's integration of artificial intelligence into its investment strategies. Dalio recognized the potential of AI in enhancing analytical capabilities and decision-making processes, thereby maintaining Bridgewater's competitive edge in a rapidly advancing technological era.

Global Political Tensions and Economic Predictions

Dalio's insights into global political tensions and their economic implications became increasingly relevant. His analysis of the US-China trade relations, European Union dynamics, and emerging economic powers offered a nuanced understanding of the global economic landscape.

Stepping Back and Fostering New Leadership

This period also marked a transition for Dalio, as he began stepping back from day-to-day operations at Bridgewater. The focus shifted to fostering new leadership within the firm, ensuring a legacy that would endure beyond his direct involvement.

Philanthropic Endeavors and Public Engagement

Dalio's philanthropic efforts and public engagement intensified. His initiatives, especially in education and ocean conservation, reflected his commitment to leveraging his resources and influence for broader societal impact.

An Enduring Influence on Finance and Beyond

Ray Dalio's enduring influence on the world of finance and his broader contributions to society. His journey from a young entrepreneur to a global influencer epitomized a life dedicated to constant learning, adaptation, and a deep-seated desire to make a meaningful impact.

CHAPTER SEVEN

BRIDGEWATER'S CULTURE AND DALIO'S PRINCIPLES

Bridgewater's Unique Workplace Culture

The unique and often controversial culture at Bridgewater Associates, heavily influenced by Ray Dalio's principles. The firm's commitment to "radical transparency" and "radical truth" created an environment unlike any other in the corporate world. This section examines both the benefits and the challenges of such a culture, including its impact on employee morale and the firm's overall performance.

The Principles in Action

From the hiring processes to the daily meetings, every aspect of the operation was infused with these ideas. Employee testimonials and case studies offer insight into how these principles shaped their professional and personal lives.

Criticism and Reevaluation

Despite the success of Bridgewater, Dalio's approach received its fair share of criticism, especially concerning the high-stress environment it sometimes created. This section addresses the critiques head-on, discussing how Dalio and the leadership at Bridgewater responded to such feedback and the subsequent changes implemented.

Global Impact and Influence

Dalio's principles extended far beyond the walls of Bridgewater. This section explores the broader impact of his philosophy on other businesses and leaders, including how other companies have adopted similar practices and the global discourse around corporate culture and leadership.

Personal Growth and Evolution

Dalio's personal journey of growth and evolution. It highlights how his experiences at Bridgewater and the feedback from his team influenced his own understanding of leadership, management, and human psychology.

A Living Legacy

As the chapter concludes, it reflects on the living legacy of Dalio's principles. It considers how these ideas have become deeply ingrained in the fabric of Bridgewater and the wider business community, shaping current and future generations of leaders and entrepreneurs.

CHAPTER EIGHT

DALIO'S PERSONAL JOURNEY AND THE EVOLUTION OF HIS IDEAS

Early Influences and Formative Experiences

Ray Dalio's influences and experiences is what shaped his character and philosophy. It looks at his family background, education, and formative experiences in the world of finance. This section aims to provide a deeper understanding of how Dalio's past informed his approach to business and life.

The Bridgewater Years: Lessons Learned

This section reflects on Dalio's journey through the years at Bridgewater. It examines the key milestones, successes, and failures, and how these experiences contributed to the evolution of his ideas and principles. Personal anecdotes and reflections from Dalio and his colleagues offer insights into his thought process during critical periods of the company's growth.

Adapting Principles to Life's Challenges

The chapter delves into how Dalio applied his principles to personal challenges, including family life and personal crises. It explores how these principles were tested and adapted in the face of real-world complexities and how they influenced his relationships and personal development.

The Intersection of Philosophy and Economics

Dalio's unique blend of philosophy and economic theory is a focal point of this chapter. It discusses how his philosophical beliefs influenced his economic predictions and investment strategies, and vice versa. This section also explores his contributions to economic thought and discourse.

Mentorship and Legacy Building

A significant portion of the chapter is dedicated to Dalio's role as a mentor and his efforts to build a lasting legacy. It looks at

33

his relationships with younger entrepreneurs, his contributions to educational initiatives, and his efforts to instill his principles in the next generation of leaders.

A Journey of Continuous Evolution

It underscores dailo's commitment to questioning, refining, and applying his principles in various aspects of life, highlighting how his journey has been as much about personal growth as it has been about professional

CHAPTER NINE

NAVIGATING GLOBAL TURBULENCE

As the world entered an era marked by rapid technological advancement and geopolitical shifts, Ray Dalio's insights became increasingly sought after. His ability to decipher complex economic patterns and his unorthodox approach to life and leadership continued to resonate across the globe.

The Economic Seer

Dalio's predictions and analyses of global financial trends gained immense attention. He became known for his accurate foresight, especially regarding market cycles and economic downturns. His speeches and writings, filled with warnings and wisdom about the global economy, reflected a deep understanding of historical patterns and their modern implications.

Bridging Philosophies and Market

Dalio's unique blend of eastern and western philosophies, coupled with his economic expertise, allowed him to offer a distinct perspective on global issues. He often discussed the importance of understanding the cultural and philosophical underpinnings of economic decisions, arguing for a more holistic approach to global economic policy.

The Role of Technology and Innovation

Embracing the technological revolution, Dalio began incorporating advanced data analysis and AI into Bridgewater's strategies. His interest in technology extended beyond its financial applications; he saw it as a tool for improving societal understanding and decision-making, advocating for its ethical and thoughtful use.

Environmental and Social Responsibility

In his later years, Dalio increasingly focused on environmental sustainability and social responsibility. He recognized the financial sector's role in addressing global challenges like climate change and inequality. Through both personal philanthropy and corporate initiatives, he championed sustainable investing and corporate responsibility.

Preparing for a New Era

Dalio's vision for the future was not without caution. He frequently spoke about the challenges and opportunities of the 21st century, urging leaders and individuals alike to adapt to an ever-changing landscape. His message was clear: embrace change, stay curious, and always be prepared to rethink and relearn.

As the narrative moves towards its conclusion, Dalio's journey stands as a testament to the power of resilience, adaptability, and the relentless pursuit of understanding in a complex world. His legacy, a blend of economic brilliance and philosophical depth, continues to influence and inspire.

CHAPTER TEN

THE ENDURING IMPACT OF RAY DALIO

Ray Dalio's enduring impact on the world of finance, philosophy, and beyond comes into full focus. His journey from a modest apartment to the helm of the world's largest hedge fund is more than a tale of financial success; it's a narrative of relentless pursuit of understanding and an unwavering commitment to principles.

Bridgewater's Continued Influence

Under Dalio's guidance, Bridgewater Associates cemented its place as a titan in the world of finance. But more than its financial achievements, the firm's culture of radical transparency and idea meritocracy became its most significant legacy. This culture, while often debated and dissected, undeniably transformed the landscape of corporate governance and employee engagement.

Philosophies for Life and Leadership

Dalio's principles transcended the confines of Bridgewater, influencing countless individuals and organizations worldwide. His book, "Principles," became a blueprint for personal and professional growth, inspiring readers to embrace reality, seek truth, and make principled decisions.

Global Economic Thought Leadership

Dalio's role as a thought leader in global economics remained significant. His analyses of economic cycles and insights into the functioning of debt markets provided valuable guidance for policymakers and investors alike. His voice, always clear and often prescient, continued to shape conversations on global economic stability and growth.

Philanthropic Endeavors and Social Impact

Philanthropy emerged as a central theme in Dalio's later years. His commitment to education, environmental conservation, and social welfare reflected his belief in using wealth for societal good. The Ray Dalio Foundation, through its various initiatives, aimed to address systemic challenges and create lasting positive change.

A Personal Reflection

In his reflections, Dalio often spoke of his journey as one of continuous learning and evolution. He viewed his mistakes as opportunities for growth and his successes as chances to give back. His life, a blend of introspection and action, served as a powerful example of what it means to live a life aligned with one's principles.

The Final Word

As the story of Ray Dalio closes, his legacy stands as a beacon for future generations. It's a legacy defined not just by financial acumen but by a deep commitment to understanding the complexities of the world and improving it. Dalio's life reminds us that success is multifaceted - a balance of personal achievement, intellectual growth, and contributing to the greater good.

In the end, Ray Dalio's story is not just about the rise of a finance titan; it's about the journey of a visionary who dared to think differently and, in doing so, changed the world.